THERE'S A HOLE IN MY LOVE CUP

OFFICIAL WORKBOOK

The Perfect Companion to the Badass Counseling Method

Sven Erlandson, MDiv, BA

The official and only authorized workbook by author Sven Erlandson, MDiv, BA

Eksjö Yard Publishing, New York

ISBN: 979-8-99057-580-6

From the Author

Great to see you diving in with the journaling work of Love Cup! This is really the most critical piece. Always push yourself to go deeper. Write questions like 'why,' 'what was really going on inside me,' and 'what is my fear in all of this,' etc. then journal out all of your answers. Keep opening up. Keep going deeper.

You got this!!
Courage!
- Sven

Workbook Instructions

This workbook is meant as a companion guide to *There's a Hole in My Love Cup* written by Sven Erlandson and is the only official workbook authored by Sven.

The contents of this workbook align with the chapters in *There's a Hole in My Love Cup* and outline the journaling, book, and song recommendations from each chapter. Additional, workbook-only content has also been included for consideration and further reflection.

Space is provided at the end of each chapter to begin journaling, but you are highly encouraged to use an additional notebook to supplement the writing space provided.

Table of Contents

The Core

Chapter 1

Therapy just doesn't work for me!

Song Recommendation

Throughout the course of this book, I will be offering songs for you to buy and use as part of your reading and meditation process. This is heavy stuff we're chewing on in this book. And, sometimes, getting the messages through music has the effect of feeling them more deeply, experiencing them more profoundly, and engaging them more meaningfully. In that vein, I commend to your listening pleasure and spirit work the powerfully intense music and lyrics of **Evanescence**, *Bring Me To Life*.

Journaling Recommendation

Alright, now we get into some really deep work. Take out a pad of paper and pen, or sit at your laptop, or perhaps even thumb-type in the notes section of your cell phone. I'm a big believer in pen and paper, but call me 'old school.' We're going to do some heavy journaling here. If you've never really journaled, great. If you have, terrific. Doesn't matter. What we're getting into isn't journaling about the color of the sky and how pretty the trees and flowers are today. What we're journaling about is the real stuff going on inside you, the stuff you've been running from. Until you reach the state of lasting bliss, you oughta be journaling daily. Heck, multiple times a day.

The simplest way I have found to get my mind going, when journaling, is simply to write a question at the top of the page, then spend a page or ten, fleshing out my answers to that question. Just keep journaling until your mind and soul are empty, or until a new or deeper question comes up. Then go in the direction of answering that question, or even coming back to a question from days or weeks earlier.

There are no right or wrong answers, as long as you're flushing out your feelings, not just your thoughts. Both. Just keep flushing it out of you. And there are certain default questions you should always be coming back to, even if the questions of the day were something completely different. Keep coming back to the questions:

1. What do I really, really feel about this, if I were to be totally honest?
2. Why?
3. What's really eating at me about this situation?
4. Why am I so angry? So sad? So afraid?
5. What's the single biggest and most powerful FEAR driving this whole equation?
6. Is there one person I'm having strong feelings about? Who?
7. What are those feelings – anger, love, happiness, frustration, disappointment?
8. How is this hardship or pain I'm experiencing the single greatest blessing that could have ever happened to me? What are the gods trying to teach me with this pain? What am I still not learning or still resisting that the ongoing pain keeps trying to get through to me?
9. In what ways am I feeling called to be an instrument of stronger love and compassion in the world? How has the past pain – the past workouts in the spiritual gym with the badass coach in the sky – perfectly prepared me for the work ahead?

But, for today's question at the top of your page I want you to start with either these few questions or just put each of the questions (below) at the top of a different page and simply journal and journal, until you're done for this day or this moment.

1. In your journal, list the five most persistent irritants in your life. These are not the giant pain sources in your life. These are the incredibly small, yet ever-present drains on your focus, energy, or happiness that are always there. Does it annoy you when people drive slow in the fast lane? Is one of your irritants when people leave the toilet seat up? Maybe it bugs the heck out of you when people use all caps in a text or are forever inserting way too many emojis? Are you irritated because the clothes always come out of the dryer all clingy and stuck together? Does it bother you when people don't use good manners, like 'please' and 'thank you'? What are those small things that annoy you? Or, maybe, you have things that you do, or fail to do that irritate you. Does it bother you that you're always losing your phone? Maybe you forever hit your

head on things accidentally? Does it bother you that you forever let your dirty laundry pile get out of control, and then you're left one morning without clean underwear?

2. Now, write out why each of these is such an irritant and how your life would be different (be as specific as possible) if each of these, item by item, were not in your life.

3. Next, tell me the story in your journal of the single most traumatic event in your life. Use as much detail as possible, as well as the most graphic, strong, even offensive language you can, if that is what you feel when writing it. Now, this question can be a real whopper! For some people, it's an absolute stopping point, because they cannot even begin to think of what that might be. And, that's okay! If that's you, just start with something small that happened in your life that traumatized you? Was it a car accident? Did someone you care about yell at you? Were you scolded publicly? Did you have a physical accident or maybe you were hurt by an animal? Think of something that really, really stung you, hurt you, made you sad or afraid or angry, and start writing out everything you remember about that story. And, to real juice up this question, think of the *oldest* traumatic memory you can think of. Maybe the oldest you can think of is two years ago. Maybe it's all the way back to when you were two years old. But, don't get hung up on not being able to remember the biggest or the oldest. It's okay. Just do your best. Get started with what is presenting itself to you. Start there. For, as you do this, more and more, more memories will reveal themselves. Further, your soul will get the message that you can handle a little something more and something more. You will get better at processing them out of you – more confident, stronger. So, just start small. Heck, start with yesterday, if someone was rude to you and it hurt. Start there. *Just start!*

4. Lastly, journal out the one decision, above all else, you most regret making in your entire life. Now, surely, even if you had trouble on the trauma question, there have got to be regrets you have about certain decisions. So, pick one and write out the full story. Then write out what you wish you would've done and how things might've progressed differently then for you, but also what you'd have or be now, if you'd chosen differently.

Chapter 2

Becoming Truest Self and Unleashing Greatness

Song Recommendation

I love this kickass song of hope and the great opening of the soul. Download and dig this upbeat tune and monster lyrics of *Unwritten*, by **Natasha Bedingfield**. 2) Download *Till I Collapse*, by **Eminem**. It's great on YouTube with the video from the *Real Steel* movies. But the song, by itself, is monster.

Journaling Recommendation

1. Are you pursuing *ALIVENESS* or something different? Why? To what degree do you fear pursuing that which truly breathes life into your soul? Is it time to start giving your life back to you, rather than giving in to the fears that keep you far less than fully alive?
2. What are the highs and hangovers you've been stuck in for far too long? In what ways do they most drag your life down? What would true carryovers look like?
3. What is the real pain, fear, or BS belief you've been taught about yourself that you are most running from with your highs? Whose voice most rings in your head? What is the bitter, sad message they deliver to you about you and your worth? Are you ready to change it?

_____

_____

_____

_____

Chapter 3

You're Running!

Song Recommendation

Listen to these songs.

1. A great song that gets at our society's obsession with running from our problems, particularly in using drugs to run. I love this song, so intense! *Kevin* (Feat. Leon Bridges), by **Macklemore & Ryan Lewis.**
2. The singer and wordsmith, who provided the soundtrack for the most intense 10-15 years of my own spiritual journey was **Dan Fogelberg**. This song, *Ghosts*, nails the horrible and beautiful memories dripping with high emotion that we run from. They sneak up like ghosts, when we're alone, when we're relaxed, and when we're tired. And so, we run. Solitude is too scary. Idling is terrifying. Nothing will do, except to run, until we simply tire of running.

Journaling Recommendation

1. What is your preferred means of running? Are you an addict? Do you like the ponies? Jack Daniels? Maybe your poison is good ol' American over-working or over-exercising? Smoke a lot of grass? Paste your butt to the couch and binge incessantly on this Golden Age of television they say we're in? Or maybe it's just sheer busyness – constant movement and commotion? Or is it Oreos, pizza, bread, and more food? HOW are you running?
2. And now the real whopper: WHEN did you start running? I know you're going to say 'I don't know' or 'It came gradually'. And maybe both of those answers are true, but I want you to push harder. Give me an answer. Find it. When do you recall the balance being tipped? When did you really most start running?

3. And what triggered it, at that point? I mean, you didn't start running a year or five earlier. And you could've started five years later. Why did you start running from your feelings at that particular time in life? What happened?
4. From what are you running? What is the one message you can't bear to hear or look at?
5. What do you most fear in your life?
6. What feelings are you most hiding from? What is the one feeling you are LEAST likely to express in your life or most afraid to express?
7. Can you imagine not running? What are the five biggest ways your life would most be different if you were no longer running? And what's the single biggest thing that keeps you from stopping the running?

Book Recommendation

Buy a copy of the book, *The Dark Side of the Light Chasers*, by Debbie Ford. Great book for diving into the parts of yourself that you have been hiding from and most need to express, in order to become full and alive.

_____

_____

_____

_____

_____

_____

_____

_____

Chapter 4

Change Will Not Occur 'Till the Pain Gets Bad Enough

Song Recommendation

The first song recommendation I have for you is a classic that speaks right to the place in life I refer to as 'The Screw-It Point,' where you no longer care about pleasing others, no longer care about all the things that have kept you locked in an unhappy life, and no longer care about wasting your life. It is **Phil Collins's** *I Don't Care Anymore*. Buy it. Sit in it. Let it strengthen you for what is ahead. 2) The second song is about the spot of feeling like you're caught in a loop of hiccups, hardships and hurdles – longing to escape but feeling stuck in the never-ending cycle. Purchase **Eminem's** *Lose Yourself* and give it a good long listen. While we definitely get more than one chance in life, this song is still inspiring as heck!

Journaling Recommendation

1. What is the pain loop you are stuck in? In what ways is your pain growing, no matter how hard you try to stop it from doing so?

2. What is the worst part about the hell you are going through? Is it the first time through this hell, or have you been down this nearly exact same path many a time before? What is it that maybe you didn't learn the first time that you are now repeating? What is the fear that keeps you from doing it differently – living differently, really – this time? Where does that fear come from? What would be the absolute worst part if that fear came to fruition? Would it be embarrassing? Sad? Hard? Frustrating? It probably would be all of those things. BUT, would you do the grieving, the healing, the mending, for whatever time it took…and then move on with your life? Riiiiigggghhhtttt! You would, wouldn't you. So life would go on, even if it came with some pain in the meantime. Maybe

it's time to choose the pain of real healing over the pain of just continuing to walk through hell. Maybe?

3. What are you feeling, right now? Don't just say 'good' or 'weird.' Pick a feeling word. What's going on inside you? Dig deeper. Where are you at inside you? Is it time to do more healing work?

_____

_____

_____

_____

_____

_____

_____

_____

_____

_____

_____

_____

Chapter 5

Your Love Cup

Song Recommendation

Great song for you to buy and listen closely to: *Secrets*, by **One Republic**. It is so perfect a song for this topic of opening your heart and revealing your real truth, not just to others but to your own self, opening the possibility of getting your Love Cup filled, both by yourself and others. 2) The second song I commend to your listening pleasure and personal growth is *Come Talk To Me*, by **Peter Gabriel**.

Journaling Recommendation

1. If you were to put percentages to it, what percent of your life are you living radically honestly and what percent are you living in fear of opening up? Is it 30% radical and 70% fear? Or is it 60% radically honest, and 40% fear living? What is it for you? What is the grand fear, the biggest of them all, that keeps you locked in that state of fear? Or, whom do you most fear? If you were to put a face and a message to that fear that keeps you doggone miserable, who's the person and what would be the one message that would most likely come out of their mouth if you were to begin opening up more, or the one message you most fear hearing them say, or would hurt the most if they did?

2. What are the parts of you that you most fear showing to another person or most fear living on the outside, rather than just carrying around on the inside? What are the ways that you hide? Are you tired of hiding and concealing your authenticity? What would it feel like to begin to live more boldly in putting your real self out there more, bit by bit? Got the guts?

3. Which of the three missing Love Languages – revealing your real truth, listening, and asking deep questions – are you actually good at, and which could you really focus on and

improve on? Do you see the value of these three hidden languages? Have you ever experienced the power of any of these when coming from another person? What happened in that experience? What did it feel like to be truly heard? What did it feel like to have someone open up and really reveal themselves to you? Did it make you uncomfortable? Did you feel trusted? Did it somehow, almost magically, draw you closer to them? What did it feel like to have someone ask you deep questions and genuinely listen to your answers? It's powerful stuff, ain't it?

_____

_____

_____

_____

_____

_____

_____

_____

_____

Chapter 6

A Ship Crossing the Ocean

Song Recommendation
Check out the song, *Time for me to Fly*, by **REO Speedwagon**. It refers to a love relationship, but can be also used to better understand parent-child relationships, too.

Journaling Recommendation

1. How have you sought to get attention in your life? If you think back, what parts of your personality are a direct result of you trying to get attention, long ago, from those people who were important to you, or maybe just from anyone? Which of those traits you created do you not particularly like? Do you exaggerate to sound important? Do you talk too much to steal attention? Did you become loud to be heard? Did you become the joker to make people laugh and like you? Did you become super smart, so that you would be praised? Maybe you became the good boy/girl, who always did the right thing or what she was told?
2. Did you take that trait and go overboard with it, over the years? Do you do it too much now? How scary would it be to scale that back? Is it time?
3. Which of the personality traits you developed to get love or attention do you actually like about you? Maybe it's some of the very same traits listed in Question #1. Do you want to expand them?
4. Who was the person(s) you were most striving to get attention from? What was it about that particular person that caused you to so crave their attention? Did you ever get it? Are you perhaps still trying to get love and attention from that person? Do you have a long pattern of theirs staring you in the face, telling you that you ain't never gotten it and ain't about to get it anytime soon? If so, is it then perhaps time to quit

contorting your life to get it, and painfully accept it ain't never gonna come, and simply begin to finally live your life for YOU? Maybe?

_____

_____

_____

_____

_____

_____

_____

_____

_____

_____

_____

_____

Chapter 7

A Ship Crossing the Ocean

Song Recommendation

Give this one a listen; buy it. It's all about the drilling-down. It's all about your real, truest self down deep inside, yearning to come out. *I'm in Here*, by **Sia**.

Journaling Recommendation

1. What are a few examples from your past where the slightest shift in your core beliefs resulted in a dramatic shift in your actions and, thus, the results and events in your life?
2. What are the areas of your life where you most need to make a shift of a few degrees in your beliefs? What is the single biggest core belief (to the degree any one person can be aware of their own core beliefs) harming your life?
3. What would those shifts in belief look like?
4. What's the single biggest thing holding you back from doing so? What is your biggest fear in considering doing so?

_____

_____

_____

_____

_____

Chapter 8

The Wet Cement of Your Soul

Song Recommendation
I have a beautiful, little ballad for you that speaks to how we stray from twirling, how life gets lost as we abandon our true selves amid the lies that get inserted into us: *The Sand and the Foam*, by **Dan Fogelberg**.

Journaling Recommendation
Questions for your journaling, today:

1. When did you stop twirling? At what age do you remember life becoming not-pretty, heavy, unhappy, or laden with a distinct sense of being really self-conscious?
2. Why then? Why that age? What happened? What do you remember being said (or unsaid)?
3. Who perpetrated the action(s) or words that caused you to stop twirling?
4. Have you ever in your life said even word-one to that person?
5. Write a letter, today or this week, to that person. DO NOT send it; just write it out. Flush out the most powerful feelings you have about that event and all that followed in years afterward. Use the strongest, even most offensive language you possibly can. Express your anger, your rage, your hurt, your tears, your sorrow, your regret for not saying something sooner, perhaps. Say it all. What is the single biggest thing you want to say or have never said to this person? What is it you most want to ask this person?
6. I'm not saying you should, but would you ever speak to or confront this person? Why or why not? What is it you most fear most in doing so – their defense, their denial, or their indifference?

Meditate on this notion of smashing the hardened cement deep inside you that holds all of your negative self-beliefs. See yourself smashing it with a sledge hammer or dropping it into the most powerful acid and melting away forever. See yourself pouring gorgeous, fresh cement that you're going to press in or write in the most wonderful, powerful, life-giving beliefs (which we'll add throughout the book). Now, journal a bit more:

1. What is the biggest, GOOD thing you can possibly imagine being written into the cement of your soul? What would feel the best? Is it, "I am wonderful," "My life matters; I MATTER," "I am good and good enough," "I LOVE who I am and who I am becoming," "I believe in you," "I am wanted," "I like me. Heck, I love me," or is it something completely different? Why that phrase?
2. What is the single most negative thing you can think of that was pressed into the former cement of your soul? Are you ready to smash that belief and let it go forever?
3. What are five sentences that explain what that would feel like?
4. Who would be most excited for you to become who you really are? Who are the people who would be your biggest supporters? What is the one sentence each of those people would say in support of you (and make it different for each person)?

_____

_____

_____

_____

_____

_____

Chapter 9

The 3 Binary Gates

Song Recommendation
Download and listen to *Let me be myself* by **3 Doors Down**. Real spiritual stuff!

Journaling Recommendation

1. In what ways did this chapter reach up and punch you in the face? What was the most powerful aspect of this part of the book?
2. Where do you see yourself with the Binary Gates? Which of yours are closed? Is it more than one? How does it feeeel to see that these gates have been closed, perhaps even your whole life? Who closed them and how did they do it? What were the messages you received that caused the closing of the gates?
3. What were the ways in your life that you have felt unwanted or even unwantable? Which is worse for you – to feel unwanted, or to feel unwantable? Why? Is it possible these feelings were never true to begin with? Is it possible that the young version of you was a wonderful, bright, happy, cranky, rambunctious, laughter-filled, playful, contemplative, creative, intelligent person? Is it possible, your original state was wonderfully wantable and that how you were treated conditioned you to believe a total lie about yourself?
4. Have you felt for a long time that you're just not good enough? Has that one thought plagued you for as long as you can remember? Or perhaps your thought is, "I'm not worthy of love." Or, maybe you go the full-blown versions of not good enough, such as "You suck," "you're a loser," "you'll never amount to anything," or some extraordinarily painful version of those very demeaning messages. List the ways that 'you're not good (enough)' was conveyed to you. Which was the most painful of those ways? List the people who have

most conveyed those messages to you and the ways they did it. Now pinpoint who really started it all. Who was the earliest? Write out your memories and feelings of when they did it, how they did so, and how it felt.

5. And now the biggie! Do you matter? Is the real you (not just the you that serves others and has to be there for them) actually important and, especially, does it matter to YOU? How were you taught that you don't matter? Who taught you that your authentic self isn't important, because I guarantee that wasn't your native state when you were born and young. If you don't believe that your true self matters, it means someone conditioned you to believe that garbage? Who was it? Or, are you afraid to admit it, afraid to admit the truth that whomever claimed to love you simultaneously taught you that your original, real self is irrelevant and should be squashed? What's the scariest part about admitting that someone you love perhaps conveyed to you that your real self just doesn't matter? How did they do it? Write about what you are feeling, right now in the moment, as you ponder and write about these questions.

_____

_____

_____

_____

_____

_____

_____

_____

Chapter 10

Growing Rods and Video Surveillance

Song Recommendation

As a brilliant and passionate expression of this loneliness and sense of hopelessness that come from living inside yourself and living with this never-ending sense of dread and failure, I commend to your listening pleasure *Don't Give Up*, by **Peter Gabriel**. Buy it and dive into the words and power.

Journaling Recommendation

1. Have you become an expert at reading people? Are your cameras always on, observing what this person wants or wants you to be; monitoring what that person doesn't like or would reject about you?

2. How much are you choking down the real you, for fear that if you asserted yourself or expressed the truths of your voice you would be unwanted or pushed away?

3. Have you become an extreme giver – a people-pleaser to the nth-degree – because you were taught to believe that you don't matter and because you so want love and to fit in, or to be given attention? Do you go waaaaaay out of your way to make people like and want you, such that you've perhaps become utterly neurotic in reading every last want of others?

4. To what degree are you forever monitoring and haranguing yourself over your words, actions, and looks, forever convinced that you're just one giant screw-up? Or, maybe it's subtler with you. Maybe you don't totally hammer on yourself, but just pick, pick, pick away at yourself, always pushing yourself to be even perfect-er, more composed, more impenetrable in your right words, right actions, right dress, right choices, and everything else, so that no one can ever find any opening, whatsoever, to criticize you. What are the ways you pick at yourself? Have you gone to the extremes in your reading of people and self that you even condemn yourself

for your thoughts? Do you see how this is not a good thing, and it's not okay that someone(s) has caused you to hate yourself so much, or even at all? At what point do you maybe begin to show yourself some compassion on all of this stuff, the compassion you were not, or are not, given by those who claim to love you or care about you? When do you begin to meet your own needs in the quest for love and compassion?

Bonus Track

Check out Bonus Track 2: *Why Telling An Adult 'Just Get Over It And Move On' Is The Dumbest Thing Ever.*

_____

_____

_____

_____

_____

_____

_____

_____

_____

_____

Chapter 11

Empty Love Cups Produce Relationship Camels

Journaling Recommendation

1. In which relationships in your life are you investing way more than you're getting? Have you become an extreme giver? Do you tend to attract extreme takers, or they attract you? How old has that gotten for you?
2. More importantly, are you beginning to understand the correlation between core beliefs and the shape of the world around you, the world you've created? Are you beginning to understand that even the slightest shift in core beliefs is a shift in the tectonic plates underneath your life, creating earthquakes of change in your life principles and eventually your actions?
3. Which relationships have you been sucked back into by shiny baubles and grand promises? How long did it take for these 'changes' to peter out? What do you think caused them to peter out?
4. From whom did you learn how to be a Relationship Camel – the person who taught you how to live with a taker and make a taker happy? And who was the taker in that Camel's life – the taker you, yourself, likely still fear critique from and long for praise from?
5. How bad does the pain of deadness have to get before you're finally ready to let go, become unwound from the emotions of others, and finally live not just freer but lighter? When do you finally realize the futility of 'happiness by proxy'?
6. 'How can I love you for you really are, if you won't show me who you really are?' Are you still hiding behind your walls? Has your pain gotten bad enough that you're willing to risk and open up?

Chapter 12

The Bag of Rocks on Your Back

Song Recommendation

The language is a bit coarse, but the message is so passionate, strong and beautiful. Please buy and listen to, over and again, *F**kin' Perfect*, by **Pink**. It's SUCH a great message!

Journaling Recommendation

1. How much life energy have you been drained of, because you've been carrying around the rocks of past pains and brutal messages about yourself that were never true to begin with? Can you name each of those rocks? Do so. Name, also, who gave those rocks of hurt and bad messages.

2. What are the emotional charges that are attached to each of those rocks? List the charges. Sadness? Rage? Betrayal? Disappointment? Melancholy? Hubris? Self-loathing? Begin to journal out everything you can think of about those rocks and the emotional charges. One surefire way to identify emotional charges is to think of all of the things in your life that trigger you. Do you understand that the things outside of you are electrifying some memory/trauma that *is being triggered?* It is those emotionally charged memories – those rocks! – that are being triggered and setting you off. So, what triggers outside of you do you shy away from that are indicators of the emotional charges inside of you? Can you name those emotional charges and where/when they began. Do so here.

_____

_____

Chapter 13

Who Owns You?

Song Recommendation

On this notion of ownership there is no better song than the little-known one by my all-time favorite group, **Chicago**; download *Feel (w/ Horns)*.

Journaling Recommendation

1. So, who is it? Who owns you, or at least a sizable chunk of the real estate inside your brain and person? What do you think of that? What does it feeeel like to know that so much of your life is either infected by or outright driven by the whims and fiat of another person? More specifically, drill down to the exact answer to this question: What percentage of your life is driven by, influenced by (perhaps even against your will), or subtly infused with the will and wants of another person or others? Conversely, what percentage of you is actually you? You okay with that?

2. What is the hardest part about realizing you don't own you fully? What are you feeling right now? Write it out. How much do you hate feeling this way and knowing you're not being you and likely have been living this way for a very long time? Ugh.

3. What would it take for you to begin reclaiming the real estate inside you, to begin shutting down the 'land grab' that has been happening for decades in your life and self? How scary is it to consider standing up for yourself *and not backing down?* Does the thought of doing so terrify you to your bones? But is it necessary, finally? Has your pain finally – FINALLY! – gotten so bad that you're sick of living as not-you and you're so ready to embrace even the painful battle of reclaiming you, even knowing there may be losses and that

may include people you care about and always thought cared about you? Is it finally time?

_____

_____

_____

_____

_____

_____

_____

_____

_____

_____

_____

_____

_____

_____

_____

Chapter 14

Y'KNOW WHAT YOUR PROBLEM IS!?!?!?

Song Recommendation
I just like this song and its message. It fits quite nicely at this juncture. *All In All*, by **Lifehouse**.

Journaling Recommendation

1. List each person in your past or present who has contributed to or reinforced your belief that you have a problem or are the problem.
2. Next to each person's name, list the specific phrases or messages they spoke to you that conveyed this message.
3. Now list next to each of those names and statements how each one made you feel.
4. Now write down all of the feelings you are feeling, right now, as you think about these people, events, and concomitant feelings.
5. Write a letter or email to each of these people, expressing in the strongest terms possible precisely how you feel. Don't hit 'send' or attach a stamp and put in the mailbox. The purpose of the exercise is to flush out the feelings.
6. Which of these people are still in your life?
7. Is it time to start cutting them out of your life, or at least start radically cutting back their impact and influence in your life?
8. Are you ready? Do you have the courage to do so?
9. Can you see the need for doing so?

_____

_____

Chapter 15

"Are you sure?" His Mother Asked, All His Life

Journaling Recommendation

1. So, what are the core beliefs causing you to question, dislike, and distrust yourself, your life decisions, and your own intuition?
2. What have you lost, as a result of not trusting your intuition in a key moment? What did that feel like?
3. What does that make you want to do, moving forward?

Bonus Tracks

To keep moving forward with the Core of the Badass Counseling Method go ahead to the next chapter. For those looking for more insights and deeper challenges, check out these Bonus Tracks:

- Bonus Track 3: People Shout Loudest When Feeling Heard Least
- Bonus Track 4: Naming The Beast Is Half the Problem
- Bonus Track 5: Pouring Out the Love Cup onto The Ground
- Bonus Track 6: The Greatest Fears in Life

_____

_____

_____

_____

_____

Chapter 16

We Are Constantly Being Led to Higher Ground

Song Recommendation
Take a listen to *Kyrie*, by **Mr. Mister**, while reading the lyrics. The sound is sweeping, high-spirit 80's rock. The message is strong: both a nod to the Christian sub-ritual of Confession and Forgiveness and, more importantly, testament to the calling of the soul to go down into yourself and the core of your experience and truth.

Journaling Recommendation

1. What are you clinging to? What age-old, perhaps tired part of your life do you refuse to let go of because it gives you some, likely false, sense of security? Does it really provide any real security, anymore?
2. What is it you know but aren't living? What's the single most terrifying part of beginning to live who you really are? And if that happened, would you survive, grieve, and move on with your life?
3. Who are you most afraid of? Whose words and influence are still controlling your life, keeping you clinging to lower ground and an unfulfilled life? What are the exact words, in one sentence or less, that they could say that you presently think would just kill you? But…would they kill you, or would you survive, grieve, and move on?
4. Has your will reached a point where it can no longer push, no longer get any further? Has your soul finally ground your will to a halt? Does this frustrate the heck out of you that you have no willpower left? Are you ready to finally submit to the calling of your soul? List all that would go into you beginning to live differently, as well as all the feelings that would accompany that? Are you ready to finally start living by the direction of your soul and most authentic self?

Chapter 17

"When Did You Know?"

Book Recommendation

A few years back, I fell in love with a particular chapter in a particular book, because it so well explicates a concept I had been selling in my normal, rough-hewn way, for years. This author does such a brilliant job of explaining this concept of listening to your body – i.e. intuition – and how it reveals your truth. May I strongly, strongly recommend the book *The Intuitive Way: The Definitive Guide to Increasing Your Awareness*, by Penney Peirce, in particular Chapter 6: Hearing Your Body Talk, specifically the section titled *The Sensitivity Scale*. Here's a tiny snippet from the book:

"...by learning to absolutely trust your body's first response, you will find the guidance you get is high quality. Goethe said these deceptively simple words: "Just trust yourself. Then you will know how to live" (p105).

Journaling Recommendation

1. When did YOU know? When did you know that this relationship, this career path, this family relationship, this geography, this personality trait, or what have you just wasn't right, anymore? How long ago did you really have your first inkling that, yeah, this ain't gonna work? And what's the real reason you didn't listen?
2. List all of the fears that kept you spinning and spinning further down the toilet, further into the mountain of pain this situation has become?
3. Put into words what this mountain of pain has really become. What is the most painful part of all of this? Why has it zapped your energy so badly?
4. Are there any areas in your life where you have actually begun to listen to your inner voice sooner than full-blown, outside shouting voice? What brought you to doing so?

Where are the areas of your life that you need to be backing it up and listening to that voice/whisper even sooner? Has your life gotten so bad enough times that you can not only see but actually know where this thing is going if you don't listen to that voice?

_____

_____

_____

_____

_____

_____

_____

_____

_____

_____

_____

_____

Chapter 18

Your Addiction to Busyness and
The 3 Steps of the Spiritual Life

Song Recommendation

Listen and dive into the song *Hold On Loosely*, by **.38 Special**. The band is singing of love of a woman, but the words are so easily converted into the love of something you consider your baby. Perhaps it's a dream, a business, a career, a passion, your art, your child, your family, or something else that is massively important to you. One of the grand challenges of life is to simultaneously hold on to and let go of that which we most want. It is so easy to kill that which we most want by holding on too tightly. It is easy to spin ourselves in circles and tie our stomach up in knots by trying to seek control and force results, always limited to just one vision of what the ending must look like.

The master of the spiritual life lives something different. It is to live in a state of trust, a state of letting go, a state of not needing exact, particular results in order to be happy. It's a monster challenge, but so gratifying when it is mastered or even endeavored.

Journaling Recommendation

1. What was the message you were taught about quitting? Is it possible that quitting can actually be a good thing? If so, what would you most like to quit? What new directions would you most like to take? What would that feel like?
2. Which part(s) of the soul journey do you struggle with most – the feel/hearing, the attack/heeding, or the quit/letting go of trying to control results? Why? What's the most terrifying part about that aspect of the spiritual/soul journey? Whose voice or presence in your life makes it so doggone hard to do it? What would it take for you to finally do it, anyway? To what degree do you need to find that 'Screw it' mentality and just do it anyway?

3. Which is harder for you, quitting or holding on loosely? How much of your overthinking and controlling is driven by the fears of everything not being 'just right'? And what is the grand terror if everything isn't just exactly the way you said and planned? Would it be possible to begin living with room in your life plans for the Universe to lead you in new directions? Would you be willing to listen to that inner voice if it were leading you to a new path that could make you even happier and more fulfilled than the safe path you are on? Is it time?

Bonus Tracks

Core readers: Move on to the next chapter.
Advanced readers: check out these Bonus Tracks:

- Bonus Track 7: The Dog and The Electric Fence
- Bonus Track 8: The Purpose Of The 'Why'

_____

_____

_____

_____

_____

_____

_____

_____

Chapter 19

Every Morning, Life is Whispering Two Questions in Your Ear

Journaling Recommendation

1. Who are you? Who are you not? The path to discovering who you, just as importantly, requires discovering who you're not. Have you given yourself enough room and time in life to just step up to the buffet of life to taste and sample things, paths, pursuits, plans, purposes, and people to discover what you like and don't like, to discover what breathes life into you and what sucks life out of you? Have you given yourself permission to just try stuff and quit if it doesn't enliven you and energize you? Have you shaken off the shackles of the nonsense notion "Don't ever quit anything" to give yourself ample berth to just play with life and see what truly tickles you and really holds your attention at this point in your life? So, what new things might be fun to try (even if you later quit them)? When do you fully realize that you only live once and that you might as well dive in and make it YOUR life?
2. What is the longest and most complete identification and definition you can give of yourself?
3. Do you have the courage to finally be who you really are?
4. Lastly, what, or who, is the biggest obstacle to you being, saying, doing and becoming that which you most fully are? What's the grand fear that accompanies that obstacle? Any chance you could do it, anyway, and no longer let fear drive your life?

_____

_____

_____

Chapter 20

How Do I Become Me When I Don't Even Know Who I Am?

Song Recommendation

By the time the late-90s rolled around, I had two young children. As a result, Disney movies were a staple in my life. And, I gotta say, I'm a fan. Pretty much love 'em all. Love the stories, the characters, and especially the music, because they're loaded with great messages, far more than just advancing the particular story line of the particular movie. Recognizing that, purchase the song *A Star is Born*, from *Hercules*. It's an upbeat song with a fitting message that speaks to the frustration of not knowing the way but discovering that the map is inside you; your heart knows the way. And while that's a giant cliché, it's also a giant truth. Give it a listen.

Journaling Recommendation

1. What have been the 3 primary paths you've gone down that were not-you or no longer are you?
2. Okay, now the telling part. What were each of the three paths sent to teach you, both about life and about you? What would you not know about you, or what would you not presently be, if you had never gone those directions?
3. In a previous chapter you assessed the difference between your parents' values and yours. Can you see now more clearly how identifying your own voice and values is critical to living your own path? In what ways?

_____

_____

Chapter 21

Diamonds and Raw Sewage

Journaling Recommendation

1. Find a relaxing place and begin to sketch out, in great detail, your lists of Diamonds and Raw Sewage.
2. At the top of your journaling pages write the question, "Who or what are all of the people or things that have power over me? What are the internal demons and external power sources that I have not yet named but still have influence over my life?" And, "Why do I keep giving them power over my life?" and "Am I ready to take that power back and start running my own life, more and more? If so, in what ways, specifically?"
3. Go back to the list of 'Stops' in the *Spiritual Life Imperatives* section. For each section, list as many things as you can that you need to stop.
4. In a relaxed position and mental state, visualize bright, white, sparkling, healing streams of light and energy flowing into your body, driving out all impurities and wounds, and exploding the grip of demons, negative energy sources, and power imbalances in your life. Breathe in and visualize all those 'stops' leaving your body and leaving your life, floating away forever.
5. Now visualize the new life of the real you bursting up and out of you from deep within, cascading through and over your life with joy, happiness, and peace.
6. Whisper your mantra to yourself, this week, "I am free, happy and alive. Negative energy is shrinking. Positive and beautiful energy is expanding from within me."

Bonus Tracks
Core Readers: Press on to the next chapter.
Advanced readers:

- Bonus Track 9: Non-Negotiables, I-Don't-Give-A-Craps, And The Power Of Percentages
- Bonus Track 10: When Positive Energy Sources Turn Negative

_____

_____

_____

_____

_____

_____

_____

_____

_____

_____

_____

Chapter 22

The Computer Chip of Your Soul

Song Recommendation

This song, more than almost any other, has been so elemental to my own spiritual life. When I was in the deepest part of the dark forest, this song spoke to me. That was a very long time ago. Yet, this absolute poetry of **Dan Fogelberg's** verse still moves my soul. Listen to *Nexus* and pull up the lyrics, as well, so that you can dive into them as he sings. It's a beautifully powerful song. It speaks to the frustrations of the spiritual path, as well as the belief that there are forces guiding our steps, speaking to us, moving us.

Journaling Recommendation

1. Whose chip(s) are you still wired into? In what ways? How scary is that? How scary is the thought of de-wiring yourself from their chip?

2. If you're a parent, what are the ways you're still keeping your children wired into your chip? Do you like the control? Do you claim it's "for your own good" or perhaps "I'm just doing it to protect you?" If you were to be reeeeaaaaalllllyyyy honest, what emotional want of yours is being gratified by keeping your child living your way, under your thumb, doing your bidding, or taking your 'advice'? How much are you using your child to get your own emotional rocks off or to quiet those roaring dragons inside you from your own bitter or hurtful past? At what point do you begin to give the child their life back? At what point do you begin to ease them back into their own power, trusting them to run their own life? Do you have the courage to keep encouraging them to trust their own chip, even when they fall flat on their face, or are you forever fixing them, correcting them, criticizing them?

3. What might be written on your chip that would be fun to explore/try/entertain if for no other reason to just see how it feeeeels and see if it's something you want to be a part of your

life more regularly? Do you have the courage to begin to explore your own chip and de-wire from the BS of living on somebody else's, even if it means them being mad at you, disappointed in you, or walking away from you? Do you matter enough to you to begin to live your authentic self with full-on *ALIVENESS???*

Bonus Tracks

Core Readers: Keep moving, right on to the next chapter.
Advanced Readers:

- Bonus Track 11: Effortlessness And Flow

_____

_____

_____

_____

_____

_____

_____

_____

_____

_____

_____

Chapter 23

Your Life Messages, Part 1

Journaling Recommendation

1. So, what were the most powerful messages you received, growing up?
2. And, as you consider those messages you received, begin to poke around and consider what the real underlying messages were. Remember, a child's mind converts all messages, even the most benign, into some judgment of his or her existence. Do you remember the NCAA coach in Chapter 15 ('Are you sure?'), and how that message of his childhood undermined his successes as an adult?
3. So, what were the underlying messages? Usually the underlying messages are some derivative of:
   o   You're not wanted.
   o   You're no good, or not good enough.
   o   You don't matter.
4. What does it feel like to see these conveyed to you in your past? How have those core messages undermined your life?
5. Do you desire to have those messages removed from your life and replaced with new, life-giving ones?

_____

_____

_____

_____

_____

Chapter 24

Your Life Messages, Part 2:
The Golden Child, The Sibling, and the Special-Needs Kid

Song Recommendation

Listen to the great 70s classic song (and lyrics), **Lonely Boy**, by **Andrew Gold**. It speaks so perfectly to the lament of the sibling of the Golden Child.

Journaling Recommendation

1. Which parent committed the greater crimes in your life? And what were the crimes?
2. Were you a Golden Child, Problem Child, the sibling of one, a disabled child, or the sibling of one?
3. What was the role of the 'other parent' in your life?
4. What got normalized in your life that never should have?
5. Is your Love Cup full of rocks and sludge? Or does it have holes in the bottom? Both? Or was there never anyone who wanted to pour love into your Love Cup?
6. What, or who, has kept you alive this long, despite the empty Love Cup?

_____

_____

_____

_____

Chapter 25

Your Life Messages, Part 3:
"The World is Your Oyster"

Journaling Recommendation

1. What were the explicit positive messages told to you by the primary power sources and love sources in your life?
2. What subtler messages or events came at other times that either completely undermined those explicit messages or chipped away at their truth?
3. What are the parameters your parents have set in place for your life that you can't transgress, no matter what oyster you're pursuing?

_____

_____

_____

_____

_____

_____

_____

_____

Chapter 26

The Truth is Obvious

Journaling Recommendation

1. What is the single biggest problem in your life that you are still trying to solve, understand, or figure out? Write it down. Now, when did it start? But, is it possible it started even before that? When did you first start to have the slightest whiff of something going afoul? Or, what's your earliest memory of something being significant and present? Is it possible that, prior to that, it had actually been building up for quite some time? So, when might it have *really* started? How does it feel to know it has probably been going on that long?

2. Now, as you consider that origin time, why then??? What happened then? I mean, why didn't it start two years earlier or 4 years later? Why then? Something happened. What was it? And, how are you feeling now to realize that? How does that alone offer new insight into what's going on today or what you feel about the whole thing?

3. If the truth is obvious, what is the obvious truth(s) staring you in the face that you just haven't been able to see, 'til now? What is it about that truth that either excites you or terrifies the bejeebers out of you? How have you missed (or avoided) this truth? How does writing about it feel? Why?

_____

_____

_____

_____

_____

The Turn

Chapter 27

The Pilot Light of Greatness Burning Deep Inside You

Song Recommendation

Listen to and meditate on the lyrics to *Take Me to the Pilot*, by **Elton John**. I'm quite fond of the extended version, 'Live at the Greek Theatre (1994)'. **Ray Cooper** is monster on percussion. In fact, I'm writing this chapter (and others in this book) with that video playing in the corner of my computer. Terribly inspiring! 2) Also, a great song from **Queen**: Listen to *A Kind of Magic*. It really speaks to this notion of the flame of greatness burning inside each one of us.

Journaling Recommendation

1. What are the ways you know your pilot is still burning, even when it feels like it's not, at times? How does it feel, even if it's just a momentary feeling, to know that it still burns, that somewhere in you is still the passion to live, quiet as it may be?

2. Have you ever been to the 'suicide point'? How long were/are you there? What was/is the worst part? Can you begin, just begin, to journal out all of your feelings on it, right here, right now? As a person who has been where you (albeit for likely different reasons), can you trust me when I tell you, I know for fact that deep inside you you still want to live? I don't care how depressed, beaten down, abused, taken advantage of, taken for granted, frustrated by closed doors, and scorned and shunned you have been, I know you still want to live. I guarantee it. Now, are you willing to trust, as well, that there is a way out, that you can actually begin the work of digging your own way out (and you can get help with it, too)? I know it seems profoundly daunting. I know it feels like too much. But, let's be really honest, you have no choice. You have to begin the work of healing yourself in ways that you have not

before, because it beats the heck out of the state you are in! There is hope. This is very, very doable. You just gotta commit and do the work to begin the healing process. And I'm telling you as a matter of absolute fact, it doesn't have to take forever, if you have the courage to go deeper into the pain and harder into the doing of the work of flushing it all out. YOU CAN DO IT!!!!!

3. Even if you're not a person at or near the suicide point, are you ready to begin the climb and the challenge of becoming into your true greatness? Are you ready to begin the transformation? What are the opening steps? What are the obstacles you need to begin addressing first? It's time!

_____

_____

_____

_____

_____

_____

_____

_____

_____

_____

_____

Chapter 28

Three Things Happen as You More Become Your Truest Self

Journaling Recommendation

1. Who are the people you are most likely to get blowback from if you were to, more and more, be, say, do, believe, and become who you really are?
2. In this list, circle the people you are most afraid to lose.
3. Write out the three main reasons for each person why you are afraid to lose that person.
4. Who on your list do you not fear losing? Do you not fear losing them because A) they would not leave you, if you were to more and more become yourself; or because B) you simply are not afraid of living without them (or without their diminished presence in your life)?
5. Write about what it would feel like to lose these people.
6. This is a very simple question: Could you live without the people you've circled? I'm sure it would be hard to lose them, but, in the end, could you live without them (or with their diminished presence)?
7. Does it change your perspective on more fully becoming your truest self to know that, in the end, you can accept, live with, and move on from the loss of any of those people? How?
8. Does it change your perspective on living your truth to know you'll begin to attract new people, who are better suited to who you're becoming?
9. What type of person – what characteristics – would you most love to attract? What would make your heart sing?

Bonus Tracks
Core Readers: I recommend you check out Bonus Track 12 with the Advanced Readers. I think you'll like it. Then come back and move on to the next chapter.

Bonus Track 12: Words Speak Louder Than Actions, Not Vice Versa (This is a really great read that I strongly recommend. It's about the broken heart of a cop, named Speedy.)

_____

_____

_____

_____

_____

_____

_____

_____

_____

_____

_____

_____

_____

Chapter 29

Jumping Ship

Song Recommendation

Listen to *Place in this World*, by **Michael W. Smith**. Beautiful power ballad that is so apropos to this notion of the Divine Spark burning deep inside each one of us, particularly when we consider that at our deepest depths our own truest voice is indistinguishable from the voice of God, himself. And it is that true Divine voice that gives us direction, gives us hope, and gives us solace when our heart most longs for reprieve from the pain and longs for the possibility of true and lasting joy.

Journaling Recommendation

1. What is the ship of security you're clinging to? What is the fear driving the clinging? Is that ship sinking, on fire, and reeking of the manure it has been hauling? And yet you still cling? What's the scariest part about diving in and simply learning to tread water, and maybe even enjoy the great freedom and adventure of it all? And what if you keep clinging and a new ship never comes, or it's worse than the one you've been on? What if you get in the water and discover there's not just one new ship, but a whole flotilla of different boats? How are you going to decide which is best for your most authentic self? Or, are you just going to pick the prettiest one, or the first one that shows you any interest, or the easiest one? How can you begin to discern the proper boat for you if you don't even know yet who you really are?

2. What are the rituals in your life that feed you? List them. Which are the rituals that bleed you, that maybe once comforted you and smoothed your way, but now are dead for you but you cling to them, maybe because you fear the unknown? What might be new rituals that could infuse your life with new vigor and color?

Chapter 30

Every Decision in Life Boils Down to Two Things

Journaling Recommendation

1. What are the five scariest things you would have the most trouble letting go of in your life?
2. What is the scariest part about trusting that, no matter what happens, you'll be okay? Why?
3. What are the ten parts of who you are that you most fear revealing to others and to life?

_____

_____

_____

_____

_____

_____

_____

_____

Chapter 31

The Power of the Third Path

Song Recommendation

I'm a big fan of this song, by **Queen**. It both inspires and well-defines clarity of purpose, which is precisely what comes when you have the courage to go your Third Path, when you have the courage to be original and follow the calling of greatness from the pilot light of your soul. Listen to and savor the tune and message of *One Vision*.

Journaling Recommendation

1. Which path have you spent most of your life on, the first or the second – shoulds or 'Screw You'? Which are you on now? Is your greater instinct to conform and do what's expected of you or to rebel and take the 'Path of the Middle Finger'?
2. Do you have the courage to begin to cut a new, third path?
3. What would the third path look like, for you? What's the first scary step?
4. What's the scariest part about carving your own path where there presently isn't one?

_____

_____

_____

_____

_____

_____

Chapter 32

"You'll Know"

Journaling Recommendation

1. This may sound like an incredibly dumb question. However, if you were to be totally honest with yourself, right now, in your journaling, write out the answer to this question: what is the god's-honest truth when I ask you, What do you know; I mean truly know? Not, what are you willing to admit, but what is your truth? Can you feel it, yet? Let me put it this way: what is the truth that has been there, all along, that you have been avoiding, constantly second-guessing, or simply not seeing because it was hiding in plain sight?

2. What is the great unanswered question of your life or your future? What is it that you do *not* have resolution to?

3. Is it possible that you know exactly what your truth is? Is it possible that you already know the answer to what you claim is the great unanswered question of your life? Is it possible that your problem is *not* that you don't know what your path or truth is but that you're terrified to act on it?

4. Living a truth or a new dream demands being judicious in to whom you reveal it, much as a tiny shoot coming out of the ground needs to be protected from too much sun, too much rain, not enough of both, and the constant threat of rabbits or a human shoe. In what ways do you need to be judicious in what you share about what you're being, saying, doing, having, wanting, believing and becoming? Who might do your dream/shoot harm? Can you be judicious in what you reveal to that person(s)?

5. What's going on inside you, as you consider what you really know about your life and path? What do you feel as you consider those who might undermine your new paths and purposes?

Chapter 33

Closed Doors are Greater Blessings than Open Doors

Journaling Recommendation

1. List the top five things, events, situations, or people that you have considered the biggest curses of your life, that would be almost impossible to find good in.
2. Now, under each one, write the questions: How was/is this event or person the single greatest blessing of my life? What was this thing sent to teach me about myself? About life? In what way is this learning I received precisely what I need for life, moving forward?
3. What have been the 3-5 biggest closed doors, disappointments or frustrations of your life?
4. How was each one perfect? What would you have missed out on, quite possibly, if you had gotten what you wanted?
5. Even if you never say it aloud or forgive the person who did it, what if the most wretched, horrible thing of your life was sent for your pruning – a gift from the gods? What if you simply can't see and don't want to admit the gems of wisdom it holds in its hand?

Bonus Tracks
Core Readers: Move to the next chapter.
Advanced Readers, here you go:
- Bonus Track 13: When The Soul Burps Gold

Chapter 34

Dumbest Exercise EVER... But it Works!

Song Recommendation

I'm recommending *Helplessly Hoping* here, by **Crosby, Stills and Nash**. It's a love song, of sorts, but the crossover to the relationship between you and your own soul is not hard to recognize. For those who are a bit saltier (and like rap), try the song by Minneapolis group, **Atmosphere**, *GodLovesUgly*.

Journaling Recommendation

1. What is the pain you continue to avoid? What is the part of you that you most loathe? Do you have the courage to finally sit in it and allow it to wash over you and pass out of you? Do you have the courage to change your language about that one aspect (and others) of yourself?
2. What is the single most difficult, positive thing you could possibly say about yourself to yourself? What is the one affirmation you could almost never believe? Why? What power source implanted that belief into you? I challenge you to make that affirmation the one at the very top of your list, the one you do most repeatedly.

_____

_____

_____

_____

_____

Parenting

Chapter 35

Even Good Parents Can Seriously Harm a Child's Soul

Song Recommendation

I remember this song so vividly from my childhood. I remember it striking me, even as a kid, as perhaps the single most depressing song ever, with such an incredibly powerful message. Yes, it's a song about regrets. But it is so fitting for this discussion of even great parents – well-meaning parents – making colossal mistakes *and* the reality that bad habits get transferred, quite unthinkingly from one generation to the next. Daughters raise their daughters often in the same mistaken system of beliefs and actions in which they themselves were raised, despite their efforts to do just the opposite of how they were raised; same with sons and their sons. Listen to the song and give a good long meditation on its words and meaning. *Cat's in the Cradle*, by **Harry Chapin**.

Journaling Recommendation

1. List the top 10 things you love and adore your parents for? What does it feel like to think about each of those things?
2. Now the toughie: What are the 3-4 things for which you have the strongest negative feelings toward your parents (or the one parent you venerate most)? Describe those things, events, or memories in complete detail.
3. And slightly tougher: Let it all flow; describe in the strongest language the truest, realest, and most powerful feelings you have toward your parents for each of the memories in #2. If you were to be completely honest, what is it you really feel?
4. If you have no strong negative feelings toward a parent(s), is it possible you're lying to yourself? Is it possible you're denying the truth? Is it possible your instinct to protect your parent, or the memory of your parent (and the guilt of betrayal

from doing the opposite), is so great that you'd rather deny and avoid than face it?

5. What are you honestly feeling, right this moment? What does that particular feeling tell us about the weight of this particular conversation to you?

Chapter 36

Children Love Parents More Than Parents Love Children

Journaling Recommendation

1. Do you tend to agree or disagree with the notion that children love parents more than parents love children? What do you struggle with most in the question?
2. Have you endured a lot of pain at the hands of your parent or parents? Write out as many memories as you can where you remember feeling hurt, unappreciated, mistreated, or unloved. Write out the full story. How many feelings can you list feeling in that moment and since then from that experience? How does it feel to know that you have been storing so many pained memories?
3. Have they made you feel guilty? Do you feel guilty even discussing the things they've done that hurt you? What messages did you receive from them or others that you're bad or wrong for saying anything negative or critical of them and how you were treated?
4. Have you been afraid of disappointing them, standing up to them, speaking your truth, or hurting their feelings? What are the things you would like to say? Have you been taught to believe that you would lose their love and support if you did stand up to them or just even admit to yourself all that you went through from them? Go ahead and journal it all out now.
5. Was love withheld from you even if you didn't do anything wrong? In what ways was the love conditional? Were you ever just loved for who you are, rather than for what you could do or were expected to do? What has that caused you to believe about yourself, perhaps that love always has to be earned and that you always need to be doing more, more, more to win people's love, because you're not lovable just the way you are? How does that feel? What does it make you want to do to change it?

Chapter 37

Grandma Charlotte's Wisdom on Parenting the Soul

Journaling Recommendation

1. Are you parenting deliberately, or are you simply doing that which your parents did? Or just the opposite of what they did? (Neither of the latter two are true deliberate parenting. Neither is parenting's Third Path.)
2. What is it you know you're screwing up on in your parenting? What do you know you need to change to begin to parent more deliberately? From what to what?
3. Do you have the courage to change?
4. Do you have the wherewithal and presence of mind, in the moment, to convey to your child that he/she isn't a bad person but just did a not-so-good thing? Or, are you undisciplined in the heat of the moment, such that you lash out or say something potentially hurtful to the soul of your child? Do you need to widen the amount of time between stimulus and response?
5. Are you careless with your words in your parenting?

Chapter 38

Motivation and Your 22 Year-Old Son
(Or Your 35 Year-Old Self)

Song Recommendation

I'm a big fan of this song. It's even on my workout mix. So inspiring. And it's a good swift kick in the butt for kids and parents, alike. Listen to the song and read the lyrics, *Something to Believe in*, by **Parachute**.

Journaling Recommendation

1. Many motivational writers and speakers as the question, "What would you do if you knew you could not fail?" So, write that at the top of your page, and take some time to flesh out all of your answers in your career and personal life.

2. However, I think the far more illuminating question is, "What would you do even if you knew you would likely fail, or if there were a very high probably of not succeeding?" In other words, what life path would you engage in if it weren't about the success but about the love of the work? See, this is the real question. This is the path that is going to hold your attention. No matter what path you take, you're going to have many failures, fall-downs, and screw-ups. And if you're only in it to have success, in the end, these failures will eventually blow out the flame of excitement. But if you love or believe in the work, the inevitable failures of life won't extinguish your zeal for the path. You might some day become even more interested in something else, but you'll not abandon your path simply because of hardships.

3. What are the paths you know, with relative certainty, that you do not want? What are you done with, or over? What paths, tasks, work, settings, or what-have-you are not you? Do you have the courage to no longer be them and pursue them?

Relationships

Chapter 39

Every Shared Experience is a Cord Binding Two People Together, Making Unbinding Tricky

Song Recommendation
Another intense **Peter Gabriel** song, *Blood of Eden*. Listen to it and get the lyrics, too. Really great stuff, particularly the duet in the middle.

Journaling Recommendation

1. Is it possible that you need to redefine your understanding of the word 'selfish'? Do you see that it's not just totally selfless or totally selfish? Do you understand that there are all sorts of places on the continuum of being self-giving and self-loving? Are you beginning to understand that it is both okay and very good to be self-giving and self-caring, more and more? Do you see how your happiness and peace depend upon you doing and becoming more of what makes you happy and gives you life?

2. In what ways can you do more to feed your own soul and energize you? What would just feeeeel great to be doing or doing more of?

3. Can you identify and list all of the ways you are engaged in life pursuits, paths and people that are sucking the life energy right out of you? Write them all out. Next to each one, list all of the ways these things and people make you feel. How does it feel to know so much life energy is being spent on things you really have no interest   in spending it on anymore? What would it feel like to begin to reduce, or even eliminate, those elements of your life? When do you think you will be ready to do so?

Chapter 40

Unhealthy People Come in Twos

Journaling Recommendation

1. What are you hiding?
2. In what ways do you keep the focus off yourself?
3. Why are you demonizing your mate? What are you afraid of? What are you hiding?
4. What's the biggest accusation you use to keep your partner/spouse looking bad and you looking good? Are you a hypocrite?
5. Are you ready to start being honest? Are you ready for radical honesty? Or, are you going to keep using people you claim to love?
6. Now, I'm not denying that your mate has done stuff wrong. I'm objecting to your claiming you haven't. Even more pointedly, why have you continued to *allow* it? What does that say about you? And here's the whopper: What fears in you have perpetuated you staying in a relationship you claim is awful and unfulfilling?
7. What's really going on inside of you that you are not admitting?

Chapter 41

The Impasse Between Two People

Journaling Recommendation

1. What relationship impasses exist in your life? Or, what relationship impasses have you been a part of, in the past? What has created them? What has been your role in allowing them to start and grow? Is it possible that you need to be doing more of the hard conversations? Is it possible that you are withholding truths that really need to be spoken, if for no other reason than you just need to get them off your chest and be heard? Do you have the courage to begin doing so? Has your pain gotten bad enough that you're tired of holding it all in and you're ready to start living differently?

2. What would you say if you began to speak your truth more? What would it feel like to do so? What would the likely response or backlash be? How would that feel? Likely, it's that response that you've feared all along. Are you ready to face it now and speak your truth, anyway?

3. What does it say that you're with someone who doesn't want to hear your truth or won't admit their own shortcomings or contributions to the problems in your relationship? Is that the type of person you want to be, long term? Have you been that person who doesn't want to hear the pain you have caused and doesn't want to hear what you need to do to change and become more responsible in the relationship and to the relationship? Are you ready to begin the humbling process of changing? What would that require of you? What's the scariest part? Do you have the courage to do it, anyway? Have your life and relationships gotten bad enough that you know you finally need to change? Are you ready?

4. Has it occurred to you that if you're not sharing the stuff inside you that hurts you, offends you, or that you feel needs to change in the relationship, you're actually lying to your partner? You're being fake by not presenting your real self

and your real needs. That false version of you is likely then getting a false version of them in response, or at least your relationship itself is not real because you're not being real. So, you can't say that you are doing everything for your partner or everything for the relationship. You're obviously not. You're withholding your real self, your real wants, your real needs, and your real feelings. When do you finally have the courage to stand up, speak your truth, and not back down, because you matter just as much as they do? What most needs to be said, even if they never choose to change and accept your needs and feelings?

_____

_____

_____

_____

_____

_____

_____

_____

_____

_____

Chapter 42

NCAA Possession Arrow & Death by a Thousand Cuts

Journaling Recommendation

1. Are you living as a three-legged stool? What do you need to add more of in your life to increase your joy, peace and the stability of your own sense of self and happiness? What do you need to be doing less of? How would it feel to finally begin making these changes?
2. When the possession arrow switches to you, do you tend to minimize your wants and needs, or perhaps even not speak them, at all? Why not begin to speak up and make your happiness a priority?
3. Worse yet, does the possession arrow never flip in your direction? How does that feel? What do you need to do to begin to change that? Write it all out here? Do you have the guts to stand up and not back down for your needs and wants?

_____

_____

_____

_____

_____

_____

Chapter 43

When "Should I Leave?"
Becomes "I'm Done!"

Journaling and Song Recommendation

Forgive me for asking the obvious questions (for your journaling), but:

1. Is it time to walk away? Are you done? Have you done everything you can do? If not, do you desire to still stay in it and keep trying? If so, why? What persistent hope keeps you in it?

2. Now, listen to and soak in the lyrics to **Macy Gray's**, *I Try.*

3. Does this song speak to where you are, right now? Or does it speak to where you were? Are you truly ready to walk away, knowing you won't stumble, knowing your world will not fall apart?

4. If you are still in it, if you're still in that state of inner wrangling and uncertainty, always responding, 'I don't know what to do,' when asked if you're walking away yet, then let me ask you for your journaling: What is it you haven't done yet? What is it that you still have not said, or perhaps never said? What is it you still feel called to keep doing, because you still don't have clarity? At least be totally honest with yourself: even if you hate doing it, what is it that you want to keep doing, at least for a little while longer? Because, if you don't have the clarity that you know you're walking away, it means you still want to keep holding on, keep trying, keep hoping against hope. And there's nothing wrong with that. But at least be honest with yourself about it. Now, whatever you wrote as your answers to those questions, go do those things. Truth is, that's the stuff that really scares you to do or say. But until you do, you're not ready to go and you're just treading water, hoping something magically changes.

5. Now, I want to ask you this, is it really that you don't want to let go of this relationship or that you're just plain terrified of

being on your own? If the latter, what are you most afraid of – being alone, the voices that mock you in your head when you are alone, what people will say, or the thought that maybe no one will love you now, at your age, or is it the simple logistics of making it on your own? (Btw, you CAN make it on your own, especially as you get stronger from living your truth.)

6. Is it possible, just possible, that new love can happen? What are you feeling right now as you consider all of this?

7. How bad does life have to get before you finally let go of the toxic Raw Sewage?

_____

_____

_____

_____

_____

_____

_____

_____

_____

_____

_____

_____

Chapter 44

Breakup Myths:
'It Was Mutual' and 'Let's Be Friends'

Song Recommendation

This is one of my top five favorite songs of all time. I've been listening to it my entire life. And while I've loved it immensely, I've secretly hated it, because it's about breakups; and it's hard to have a favorite song be about breakups (much like The Carpenters, *Goodbye to Love*). But, not only is this the consummation of the early, brassy yet hardrock-edged **Chicago** sound, it's a great message in this context. We're discussing the fear of breaking up, particularly the fear of hurting the other person and looking like the bad guy.

But, *Feelin' Stronger Every Day*, by **Chicago**, gives a great message about being the person who was broken up from. It's a message of hope. But it's also implicitly a message to the person considering breaking up from someone, 'Don't be afraid. Do the break up. They will get stronger. They will recover.' And if they have the courage to go into themselves, they will find that this 'no' from you was a passageway into a greater 'yes', both from their own self and from a new lover.

Back when I was an NCAA Strength Coach, a friend of mine, who was an assistant coach for one of the teams, told me that his favorite word as a coach was the word 'No.' "Why is that," I asked.

He explained, "Sven, 2/3 of my job is spent recruiting, not coaching. At the collegiate level, it's all about recruiting. On-field coaching is so greatly determined by recruiting. So, I spend hundreds and hundreds of hours, every year, calling high school kids and their families, trying to get them to come to our school. I may call a kid 20 or 30 times. One kid! Do you have any idea how good it feels to get the word 'No'? You'd think I'd hate it, and I do; but I also love it. Because, when I get a 'no' it means I can stop calling that kid. It narrows my list, not just whittling down my workload but clarifying my list. When I get a kid who has the guts to actually tell me 'no', rather than just string me along and let me keep calling him, I love that kid. I respect that so much, because it's a sign of respect for me and my time. 'No' is such a gift."

What's true in recruiting is true in relationships. The person on the other side of your 'no' will recover, get stronger, get clarity, and move on to a greater, happier state in life. 'No' is such a blessing. Feeeel the 'no'; feel what it will be like when it is spoken and moved past. Feeel the possibility of new life, new happiness, and new love.

Journaling Recommendation

1. Who really ended that relationship that you think about when you read this chapter? Was it them or you? What was the real reason for the breakup? More importantly, why have you not wanted to admit that it wasn't mutual? What is it that hurts so much or is so scary about admitting that?
2. What was it about the feeeel of that relationship, or those relationships, that turned you off and caused you to end it? Or, even if you didn't end it, what is the feeling, in retrospect, that you're glad to be free of?
3. Do you trust yourself and get out of relationships when the feel has deteriorated with no chance of repair, or do you hold on and hold on, afraid to let go? What's the scariest part about letting go? Is it possible you so fear being alone with all of the messages from your past that rise up and storm through your head and heart telling you you're not important, not lovable, and unwantable? Journal now the feelings you're most trying to avoid by holding on.
4. Have you tried to be friends with someone immediately after the relationship ended? Were you the person who was trying to get away but didn't have the stomach for making a clean break? Or, were you the person holding on, hoping to work your way back into their loving graces and having them want you? What were the fears driving you to do this? Write them out. Write out how they feel. Write about what life would be like if you were finally past them and able to be alone without fear and pain.

Chapter 45

Surprise!

Song Recommendation

Could any collection of songs be complete without Michael? So perfectly appropriate to both your evolution throughout this book and the climax of this final Love Funnel chapter, I offer this MJ classic, which speaks of self-change and commitment to serving those whose need is even greater: *Man In The Mirror*, by **Michael Jackson**.

And now, one final recommendation: the all-time classic that has been covered by Heart, David Foster and others. The original of *You're the Voice* was written and performed by **John Farnham**, back in the 80's. It's a totally kickass song. I LOVE it. Love Foster's version. Love Heart's version. But love the original most. Actually, the very, very best version is performed by Farnham live at the 2003 ARIA Awards. For, he includes timpani, bagpipes, orchestra, and a whole lot of energy!!! You can pull it up on YouTube. If you're looking for inspiration, this song MUST be part of your music library.

Journaling Recommendation

1.   Are you ready to begin living differently? What most needs to happen to do so? Are you ready to finally become free, happy, at peace, and fully experiencing *ALIVENESS???* It's time!

Benediction

And now, lastly, this:

[Spirit of the Universe],
You have called your servants
To ventures of which we cannot see the ending, By paths, as yet,
untrodden, Through perils unknown.
Give us strength

To go out with good courage,
Not knowing where we go,
Only that your hand is leading us
And your love supporting us. Amen.

--from the liturgy of *The Lutheran Book of Worship*

_____

_____

_____

_____

_____

_____

_____

_____

_____

_____

_____

_____

Bonus Tracks

Bonus Track 1

The Root of All Depression and Anxiety

Journaling and Book Recommendations

1. What are the parts of you that you're most afraid to show the world? Why?
2. In your intimate relationship, what are the three things you're most afraid to show about yourself to your partner? Why? What are you most afraid will happen? Are you afraid he/she will reject you?
3. What about in your friendships, what are the two or three things you are most ashamed of or most afraid to show people?
4. What is the one career path or life choice you most want but are most afraid to make or reveal? A) Why do you want that? What's really at the heart of wanting that? B) What is the biggest reason you're afraid to make that decision or reveal that truth?
5. How does your inner life most manifest in your outer life, as depression or anxiety?
6. Who are the 1-3 people who would most accept you and love you, no matter what you revealed about yourself? Why? How have these people won your trust?
7. Who are the 1-3 people whom you know, for fact, would most judge or criticize you, if you were to reveal more of your truths? Why? What evidence have they given you in the past that they would criticize you?

Now, if you read no other book besides this one, let it be *The Sedona Method*, by Hale Dwoskin, which details the method for de-charging your past (and present) that was created and perfected by Lester Levenson. It is a very fast, highly effective method for emptying out all the pain inside and living free and imperturbable as you go on about your life.

However, do not attempt to read the book if you're not going to follow through. *The Sedona Method* is not so much a book as a workbook. It requires the daily discipline to work the very simple formula for, say, 20 minutes per day. You can do it on your morning commute to work. If you are a person who regularly works out, goes to yoga, meditates, or engages in any other form of self-discipline, you can do the Sedona Method on your own. But, you gotta do the daily work as your spiritual discipline. If you lack self-discipline or just lack time, this book may not be the best for you, even though it is a book that is one of the top-3 most life-changing books I have ever read and used. In that case, the Sedona Method is offered as weekend workshops, which I also strongly recommend and have sent clients and members of my own family to. That, too, requires turning it into a brief daily habit (for 60 days, minimum), but it's easier to keep that habit when you've laid the foundation for it over a weekend with other people and a teacher. Whichever you use, book or workshop, I simply cannot recommend this highly enough for de-charging internal memories and emptying out the scalding and cruddy stuff from inside. If it is used everyday, The Sedona Method can and will change your life!

_____

_____

_____

_____

_____

_____

_____

_____

Bonus Track 2

Why Telling an Adult to "Just Get Over It and Move On" is the Dumbest Thing Ever

Journaling Recommendation

1. Has anyone ever told you to "just get over it" or "just let go"? What did that feel like? Were you ever able to move through and past what they told you to get over?
2. Have you ever told someone to let go or get over it? What was going on inside of you that caused you to say that? Were you frustrated with them, upset internally by their struggle, or perhaps angry? How much do your own emotions cause you to control or judge others? List some examples of when you did that, what you were feeling, and what you did. How does it feel to remember these situations? Write that out, too.

_____

_____

_____

_____

_____

_____

_____

Bonus Track 3

People Shout Loudest When Feeling Heard Least

Song Recommendation
Here's a very well-put statement by an 80's fun group, **Tears for Fears**. It's quite fitting for this work in clearing the heart of all that weighs it down. The song is ***Shout***. Give it a listen.

Journaling Recommendation

1. What is your soul longing to shout? What is it longing to say?
2. Whose voice are you trying to be heard over? Who has most stifled your voice?
3. In one sentence or less, what is the one message most being spoken to you that negates what you've been trying to say or your soul has been longing to say?
4. Do you live with a clean heart – that is, what is it in your life that is still unspoken and to whom have you not spoken your fullest truth?
5. What would it take for you to finally have the courage to speak your truths, so that your heart might finally be clean and light? Do you have the courage to do so, even knowing the price might be high?

_____

_____

_____

_____

Bonus Track 4

Naming the Beast is Half the Problem

Journaling Recommendation

1. What is the beast in your life that is still unnamed? What are the earmarks, or symptoms, of the beast afflicting your soul? How is the affliction manifesting itself?
2. It's sometimes hard to see it on our own, to go deep enough on our own, but what can you see? What is the grand fear afflicting your life? Why?
3. What is your preferred means of running from your afflictions? Is it an eating disorder, the bottle, gambling, or what?
4. What would your life look like if you stopped running?

_____

_____

_____

_____

_____

_____

_____

_____

Bonus Track 5

Pouring Out the Love Cup onto the Ground

Song Recommendation

To really sing to where you are in this space of being down, download the song and lyrics to *Away from the Sun*, by **3 Doors Down**.

Journaling Recommendations

1. When have you felt unheard or unseen? What did you do make yourself heard/seen? Did it work/help? What does it feel like to be unheard or unseen? What does it feel like when you are heard/seen? Do you have the courage and tools to speak up and demand to be seen and heard in life, especially by those close to you and/or those whom you love or who claim to love you?

2. When have you perhaps made someone else feel unseen or unheard? If you have children of any age, have you ever caused them to feel unheard or unseen? What is it that has caused you to ignore or not see another human being, particularly a child? What is going on inside you that causes you to not see them or hear them? How does it feel to know you've done that? Do you desire to change that?

3. Most importantly, are YOU hearing your own soul's voice speaking to you from within? Are you heeding it, acting on it, trusting it and where it is leading? What is the biggest fear that keeps you from trusting your own inner voice? Do you fear backlash? Perhaps you fear not being liked? If those things happened, would   life end for you, or would you grieve what needed to be grieved and then adjust and move forward with life? Would life go on? If so, then perhaps you are giving way too much credence to the fears of people's reactions when you choose to express your real self.

Bonus Track 6

The Greatest Fears in Life

Song Recommendation

Particularly for the fear of loneliness, I strongly recommend reading the lyrics and listening to the song, *Goodbye to Love*, by **The Carpenters**. I love the fuzz guitar solo at the end of the song; tight! But the lyrics soooo powerfully speak to this sense of loneliness and despair that comes with giving up on love and on oneself. I love, love, love the powerful melancholy of this song!

Journaling Recommendation

1. Which are your greatest fears of the list of fears? What is it about that fear, or those fears, that it so possesses you? What would be the absolute worst thing that could happen?
2. As you consider the worst-case scenario of the fear(s) that grip you most, how much of the fear is wrapped up in what people will think or say? In other words, how much do people's thoughts/opinions/judgments of you still run your life? How much is fear the driving factor of your life? If it is a lot, how does it feel to know that is the case? Do you wish it were less? Write as much as you can about your fears, especially this, What messages that you received in your past are the origin of this particular fear? Who delivered that message most? Do you see how that person's judgment still runs your life? Are you okay with that?

Bonus Track 7

The Dogs and The Electric Fence

Book Recommendation

The Untethered Soul, by Michael Singer. Great book! Dense and strong. Much to absorb.

Song Recommendation

Let's go country! I love this song. Such a simple message. So clear and true. ***Born to Fly***, by **Sara Evans**. Give it a good long listen. The message will stick in you and inspire you.

Journaling Recommendation

1. What invisible electric fences in your head keep you locked into a limited life that you no longer enjoy, if you ever did? What would it take to lower your shoulder and push through to the other side? What's the fear keeping you stuck? How big is that fear? How much of it is real?

2. What would you do if you didn't have the electric fence in your life? What would you pursue? How and where would you live? The question isn't just "What do you want to have in your life," but more importantly, "What do you want to do with your life," because doing means action steps. And when you know what you want to do, you can then begin to identify the fears and pains that are blocking you inside from doing it? What is your single greatest fear in going after the life you dream of? Could you move forward anyway, a bit more each day? Would your survive, even if that great fear came to pass? What would it feel like to survive it and know you have your life ahead?

_____

_____

Bonus Track 8

The Purpose of the 'Why'

Journaling Recommendation

1. What is the grand 'why' you are still trying to resolve in your life?
2. Speculate! Knowing you could change your mind in five minutes or five days, if you were to just come up with a ballpark answer, what would you guess is the answer to that why? What just sorta fits for you as the answer to that why? So, why not run with it and let that be the why, and just let go of the fears?

Bonus Track 9

Non-Negotiables, I-Don't-Give-A-Craps, and the Power of Percentages

Journaling Recommendation

1. Go ahead and do the exercise of this Bonus Track. Or, maybe you already did as you were reading or listening to it. How did it feel to come up with your answers? Was it fun to play with this exercise, a bit? What new insights did you have?
2. What did it feel like to attach the percentages to the different negotiables? Does that give you more clarity about what you really are willing to compromise or not compromise on?
3. What do you still need to think or feeeeel more about before you can fully complete the exercise?

_____

_____

_____

_____

_____

_____

_____

_____

Bonus Track 10

When Positive Energy Sources Turn Negative

Journaling Recommendation

1. Have you ever had too many diamonds? How did you have to rearrange your life to scale them back? Or maybe that time is now. Do you need to rearrange your priorities? What needs to change? What does that say about who you've become? Are you okay with that? How does it feel?

2. Why were your priorities the way they were, before? How much was fear a driver in the former ordering of your priorities? What was the fear driving that former list? How does it feel to no longer be so fully gripped by that fear? What can you do to reduce even further the grip of that fear on your life?

_____

_____

_____

_____

_____

_____

_____

_____

Bonus Track 11

Effortlessness and Flow

Song Recommendation

Growing up in the 70s and 80s, I am a very big fan of the master craftsman, **Peter Gabriel**. But that love for his music is only heightened by the enormously soulful, powerful nature of his solo work, much of which came later in his career. One of my faves, so apropos to this conversation of trusting flow and the effortlessness of life that comes from doing so, is *Washing of the Water*. It's a song written, in part, about the loss of love and the longing of the soul for healing. Yet, it's simultaneously a song about this deep notion of believing in the flow of the river of life, trust in the healing of soul waters, and, ultimately, about trust.

Journaling Recommendation

1. Have you ever experienced times of living in flow? What did it feel like? Write out all your memories of living that way? Write out the feelings that it brought?
2. What brought about those times of flow? What decisions or actions most facilitated those periods of living in flow? What do you need to do more or less of to allow for more flow in your life? What is the area(s) of life that needs the most changes in order to allow for more flow? Does that area of your life perhaps need to be eliminated entirely? Are you almost ready to do that?
3. What comes most effortlessly to you in life? Do you need to be doing more of that, or are you in a good place with that? What does effortlessness feeeel like to you? Write out times when you are living most effortlessly and what you need to do to create more of that effortlessness, ironically enough?

Bonus Track 12

Words Speak Louder than Actions, Not Vice Versa

Song Recommendation

I think **Christina Perri's** song, *The Lonely*, so so so brilliantly conveys the power of loneliness, making it very easy to understand how each one of us, like Speedy, can so easily spend our lives running from it. Fear of loneliness in the future (and the voices inside us that arise in loneliness) is so overwhelming as to make it easy to engage in all sorts of bad decisions within the context of an existing relationship. This song also highlights the fear of going inside to actually look at and remove the pain and fears. Listen to her song and soak in the powerful sound and message.

Journaling Recommendation

1. What words have you been believing to too great a degree? Why have you so wanted to believe those words? What would it feel like to let those words go and see the fullness, or absence, of actions behind them, and accept the truth of what those actions are saying? What's the fear?
2. What would feel like to live more by actions and less by the words you're hearing?

_____

_____

_____

_____

_____

Bonus Track 13

When the Soul Burps Gold

Journaling Recommendation

1. So, let's tinker around a bit here. This is generally something I have to do in person, because I have to be able to sniff out with my own curiosity where to go with the questioning. But let me ask you, if we were to set your *future* aside and only look at your *present* and *past*, what are the three biggest "I don't knows" in your life? That is, what are the three biggest things from your past and/or things you still think or do in your present that you have no explanation for, or that you have always answered "I don't know" when queried about why you do that? What are the great unanswered questions of your life?

2. Now, if you were to speculate what the answer to one of those questions is, what would you say it is? Just if you were to take a wild guess, knowing you could change your mind tomorrow or next week, what would you speculate is the real reason?

   ▪ I often have people say to me, "Well, Sven, I don't know. I've never thought about this, before." I know you haven't. I'm asking you to not only think about it now, but to stay focused on it and just throw the answer out there that it might be, just off the top of your head.

3. Now do that same thing for the other two things from your past and/or present that were your other "I don't knows." Speculate. What *might* the reasons be? Now, if I were with you, I'd be able to sense whether it's deep enough or not, whether it's the 'bingo' answer or not. But you're gonna have to do this part on your own. And it requires a certain measure of intuition and sensing and feeeeling the answer for what sorta feeeels right.

- One way to test it for veracity is to simply sit on it for a day or week. Offer up that answer and hold it. Dwell on it for a week. Let it sit back there in your head, off the front burner. Come back to it in a week and just feeeeeel again. Does it feel like that really is the answer? If you have to keep thinking about it and vacillate, back and forth, let it go. When something is right, it just feels right; there's a certain sense of knowing it's right.

- One more way to test the rightness of an "I don't know" answer is with this simple question, "Did your answer bring an epiphany? Does it feel like an epiphany? Does it feel like a 'Holy Crap!' moment? Does it give you a sense of 'Wow. Wow. Wow,' like you just stumbled upon something very real, very significant, very powerful? If not, it's not the right answer. When you hit the answer to a long-held "I don't know," you know it. You feel it. There's a serious sense of awe that you just stumbled upon something seriously ill, seriously monster.

4. What's the effect of realizing these new answers to your big 'I don't knows'? What is the vibe? Does it feel like you've just found a new door, like you've just looked inside one of the hidden secrets of life, like hardcore 'Holy Crap!'?

5. See, now's the really trippy part. Now, you gotta start spinning out the ramifications and multiple sub-epiphanies. What other revelations do your three epiphanies give birth to? What is it you realize you need to do/be/say/become/etc? What really, really, really are the course corrections that spin out of all of this? How does this re-write the story of your life, past and present? See, this is where life starts to get heavy, get real, and get deliberate. If you can dive into your own "I don't knows," you can do some serious soul-spelunking. The wisdom of life begins to not only open up to you but do so at your command. And this is when the velocity of soul work increases exponentially, when you can begin to look within, deeper and deeper, all on your own. Now is when we're getting somewhere.

Made in United States
Troutdale, OR
10/12/2024

23699121R00128